POLIKY

ME BRAIN OPEN UP

Leyton Franklin, B.F.A. Hons

outskirts
press

The opinions expressed in this manuscript are solely the opinions of the author and do not represent the opinions or thoughts of the publisher. The author has represented and warranted full ownership and/or legal right to publish all the materials in this book.

POETRY
ME BRAIN OPEN-UP
All Rights Reserved.
Copyright © 2016 Leyton Franklin, B.F.A. Hons
v3.0

Cover Photo © 2016 Leyton Franklin. All rights reserved - used with permission.

This book may not be reproduced, transmitted, or stored in whole or in part by any means, including graphic, electronic, or mechanical without the express written consent of the publisher except in the case of brief quotations embodied in critical articles and reviews.

Outskirts Press, Inc.
http://www.outskirtspress.com

ISBN: 978-1-4787-7563-8

Library of Congress Control Number: 2016910291

Outskirts Press and the "OP" logo are trademarks belonging to Outskirts Press, Inc.

PRINTED IN THE UNITED STATES OF AMERICA

Table of Contents

INTRODUCTION vii
1987 MOTHER AND HER CHILD! 1
1987 LOVE HAS ENDED 2
1989 A BAD WEEK 4
1990 LIFE REVOLVES. 6
1993 STRANGE TRIP IN A DREAM. 7
1993 GUYANESE PARTY. 8
1999 WHAT IS LIFE? 10
1999 HELP. 13
1999 FEELINGS 15
2000 ROOSEVELT BERNARD DOUGLAS 1942 to 2000 . 16
2000 DRAMA 19
2000 POSITIVE-NEGATIVE FORCES 23
2001 HAS THE CHANGE REALLY COME?. 24
2001 I AND I. 26
2001 SOME OF THE PROBLEMS IN RELATIONSHIPS . 28
2001 WOMAN, GIVER OF LIFE 30
2001 SURPRISE IN EMERGE
     WITH MOTHER AND SICK CHILD 31
2001 THE FIRST TIME I SAW YOU 38
2001 I AM A HUMAN 2 40
2001 WHY CALL ME SELFISH 42
2001 YOU DID NOT CREATE ME 44
2003 BLACK WOMAN AND MAN 45
2003 ALTERED STATE (A Caribbean Perspective) 47
2003 MY TRIP TO JAMAICA. 49
2003 IN JAMAICA EVERYTHING MOVES 52
2003 AMERICANIZED (Information Overload). 55

2003 SMILE	57
2003 INSECURITY IS KNOCKING	58
2003 I AM IN TOTAL SHOCK	59
2004 THE LOVE BUG	63
2004 BROKEN CARIBBEAN ENGLISH	65
2004 WAN TRIP PUN DE BUS IN TORONTO	68
2004 DE PLACE ME FUS WOK IN NART MERICA	70
2004 WHY IT TOOK SO LONG?	
I Must Get Out of the Cold	72
2004 CHANGES BEFORE ME EYES	76
2005 HIGHEST ACHIEVEMENTS (Through Nature)	77
2005 GETTING OVER A WRONG DONE TO YOU	80
2005 IDEAS DEVELOPED OVER THE YEARS	81
2006 JUSTIFY	82
2007 ARE WE PREPARED FOR THIS LIFE?	83
2011 YO WANT DE TRUTH BUT YO CAN'T	
HANDLE IT	84
2011 A SPACE BETWEEN US	91
2011 CARIBBEAN "GIVE ME" PROGRAM	92
2012 RESPONSE	94
2012-01-11 TODAY	95
2012 MY LIFE	97
2012 RESPONSIBILITY AT WORK	100
2012 THANK GOD IT IS FRIDAY	102
2012 THOUGHT	103
2012 TO MY LOVING PARENTS,	
WHO HAVE PASSED (On My Birthday)	104
2012 ME HOMELAND	105
2013 COUPLE ON THE TRAIN 10:00 PM	108
2013 SUNDAY 22 DECEMBER	109
2013 CARIBBEAN PEOPLE	110

2013 MOTHER/WIFE 111
2013-19 DECEMBER MANDELA 112
2014 HAVE FAITH 116
2014 GOD 117
2014 PARENTS TEACHINGS RETURN 118
2014 ABOUT A FRIEND............................119
2014 REMEMBER 120
2015 OLD AGE...................................121
2015 LIVING WITH GHOSTS 122
2015 DREAM IN TRINIDAD.......................124
2015 MOTHER OR WIFE 125
2015 IMMIGRANT LIFE...........................126
2015 SUMMER 130
2016 CHANGING CUSTOMS 133
2016 6:30 pm FRIDAY AFTERNOON................135
July 4-2016 INSECURE MAN ON THE SUBWAY 138

INTRODUCTION

According to James Baldwin, "One writes out of one thing only — one's own experience. Everything depends on how relentlessly one forces from this experience the last drop, sweet or bitter, it can possibly give. This is the only real concern of the artist, to recreate out of the disorder of life that order which is art."

The poems are a collection of thoughts which started in 1987 to present. They don't follow the European format or subscribe to stanza. They are written in Caribbean lingo and English as the information flows and with a Caribbean perspective, using words as they sound and feelings. Some are derived from dreams or developed from the mind. Others I witnessed, as in:

- Mother and son (Caribbean) in a hospital "Surprise in Emerge with Mother and Sick Child"
- Life situations "Old Age" or "Immigrant Life"
- Death of my loving parents, Rosie Douglas, and Mandela
- Trip around the city by bus or subway "Couple on the Train 10:00 p.m."
- Holiday in Jamaica expressed in poem "In Jamaica Everything Moves"
- Returning home (Guyana) resulted in "Changes Before Me Eyes" and "Caribbean 'Give-Me' Program"
- Work places
- Relationship between women and men

1987 MOTHER AND HER CHILD!

In the Caribbean breastfeeding is an open thing.
Mothers openly breastfeed babies for a cause
Mothers never see shame breastfeeding their child.
People see mothers feeding but not the breast.
Nobody worried, mind but feel happy baby feeding.
No shame.
No shame.

No Caribbean woman interferes.
No Caribbean man ever dares.
Seeing mothers breastfeeding.
It is no pain and feeling shame

North American people feel shame.
Fraid fa see mother breastfeeding
Expose feeding dem hungry pickney.
Dem feel dat it bad fo dem children see

Turn on dem husband when dem see.
Is women dem causing all de problems?
Ha-ha-ha dem feel shame.

1987 LOVE HAS ENDED

Love has ended
Before it has begun.
I have to accept it
And not reject it.
Funny
'Reach-out' and touch.
Hoping to be loved in return.

My love is real and still is.
It would be given freely.
Looking for love in return.

Will it be possible to freely give love?
Will I ever get into a state of love?
Will I ever be loved?

Could it be I am not understood?
Could it be I am looking at the wrong women?
Could it be I am too old for her?

Can I say I tried?
And it didn't work.
Does society produce loving women?
Or is it the loving family?
Is there a reason being in this world?

Love has a history of repeated hurts.
Life, a repeated history of changes
The only permanent stages we encounter
Have to encounter these developments

These stages we go through before it ends.
Searching for love before life ends.
So let's keep on trucking.

1989 A BAD WEEK

A visit I did not expect today.
But will accept it anyway.
Sundays would have been better.

Thoughts interrupted.
Thinking about life.
It was on the move.

Compiling better thoughts.
Keeping my mind active.
Achieving what I want.

Started to think about her.
Is her mind beyond her age?
Is she great at love and reason?

Is she happy to be back?
Is she proud of her race?
I don't have the answers.

Main concern was troubling.
Does she respect life?
Could she handle being loved?
Could she willfully destroy it?
Troubling
Will the relationship survive?

Survive repeated struggles.
Repeated struggles continue.
Can it be over for us?
Could we turn a new page?

Is our friendship really at rest?
Can we move to a new future?
It seems only time can tell.

Thoughts are interrupted.
Loud knocks at the door.
It is her.

1990 LIFE REVOLVES

We're a product of changes
Life was created by changes
Leaves a mother's womb
For a changing world

Leave the world of change
Into earth's womb

Came from mother's womb

Returns dead to mother earth
Woman and man create us.

Then we create a family.
Life begins at the first breath

Lose the last breath at death.

Lived first with a mother
Then live with a woman
As lover, wife and mother.

Trained by our parents
Then teach our children.
Life continues revolving

1993 STRANGE TRIP IN A DREAM

Leaving Atlanta City
Used a plane for home.
Woman in the next seat
Traveling too.

She was not alone
Her child by her side
Surprise!

She was traveling on vacation
First visit to see Toronto.
She was afraid to talk
To an African man close by
Then we got close talking.

Music was playing as we talked
Time was passing while traveling
Trip ended as the plane landed
So did the two travelers talking
Black man and White woman

1993 GUYANESE PARTY

Attended a party in a dream.
It was a sunny day in June
In a park next to a bridge
By a moving river

Everyone having fun
Dancing to popular music
Friends meeting friends
Not seen for a while.

Plenty of rum and beer to drink
Guyanese foods to eat fo so.
In the height of all the fun,
Gunshots were heard.

Everybody diving for cover
Lying on the rough ground
One man was left standing
Looking and frozen in time.

Standing male with smoking gun
Found his wife sitting on a man
He shot her dead as people ran
Was held down on the ground

Caught by two men before he ran.
Held down until cops arrived
People leaving for their home
I was held up by another man.

Held up at gunpoint to my head
By the high bridge close to the dead
He said, "Not you to be shot but another"
Surprised, he soon let me go.

Left the frozen spot in a hurry
Passing plates of food not eaten
Left on tables by people running

People could not pack baskets
Leaving the park in a mad rush
Vendors also leaving the park
Selling beer and fishcake.

Returned to the spot
Looking for my bicycle
It was not there
Gone
Stolen

Walked five miles for home
Cannot understand this dream.

1999 WHAT IS LIFE?

Did you know my face?
Surprised

Connection was made
Facial traits

Met my father
Had not seen for a time.
Surprise!

Meeting was cold.
Got a menthol cigarette.
It was unfinished

He went for a bath.
No surprise.

Mother didn't see me
Entering the kitchen.

Hugged her from behind.
Moving from side to side
Not a word spoken
No surprise!

She was happy
So was I.
She left the kitchen

Family getting dressed
Attending a party
Surprise!

Father was always the last
Getting dressed
Anytime.
Attending an event.
No surprise.

Rose was visiting.
Somehow,
We walked for a mile

Fetching a bucket of water
For the home
Another surprise!

The bucket had a hole
Plugged it with soap
She was amazed.
Don't know why

Don't know why
She grew in the bush.
Surprise!

Arrived at family gathering.
Nobody expected me.
All were surprised.

Met a brother with colored hair.
Busy talking with the ladies.
No surprise!

This is no surprise!
Party filled with family.
All young people
Holding children.

Strange.
Smoking menthol
I got from my dad
A female joined me smoking

She didn't know who I was.
Started crying after knowing
Had a breakup with her man.
This is no surprise.

I suddenly wake
Left wondering
Why?

My parents are dead.
Rose and I parted.
Don't know my young family.
What is the dream telling me?

Never forget my brothers.
Why should I?
Didn't see my loving sister in this dream.
Why?

1999 HELP

I need help!
Spiritual help
I was told.

Along a spiritual road
Living a spiritual life
I didn't understand

Who will be my guide?
Is one needed?
I can find my way

Teaching from without.
Building the perfect way.
Creating a perfect way.

Will the teacher have faith?
Is the teacher a perfect one?
Along the international highway
But are they perfect?

I am a perfect teacher too
I can teach myself the way.
Become a perfect living soul

Full with knowledge and love.
The inner soul will be a teacher
Help from the inner teacher

So let it be.
It takes time
Inner teacher knows
Becoming productive

New relationship grows
Learn to support each other.
Follow the inner teacher.

I will know.
I will grow
Listen

Learning stages to success
Starting on a road to success.
Enjoy
Good luck

Your life is in your hands.
Just have to do the best
Working with the soul.

1999 FEELINGS

A great person and feeling great
Believe in the Creator and happiness.
Will eventually enjoy what life has to offer
Will there be financial independence?
Will be in a better position.
Will be better at networking with people.

2000 ROOSEVELT BERNARD DOUGLAS 1942 to 2000

Who was Rosie
As he was called?
Few people knew

We knew his bravery,

Lovingness, and giving

The rest only knew his name.

Remembered Rosie
As a political leader
An educator
Fighting for a change
In their educational system.

Remembered Rosie
As a friend
Devoted to helping others
Struggling for fair treatment
And equal justice for all.

"THEY" called him
A radical
Ex-Marxist
A destructive student
A political protester
They trained him, so what.

"THEY" called Rosie
A political threat
To their security
They jailed him for 18 months
After they deported him to his country
Later he became a Prime Minister.

"THEY" always get away with it.
Did Rosie?
No, they didn't agree with him
Even if you aren't guilty
"THEY" say you are.

Replying, Rosie stated,
"It was a historic event"
"I'm not ashamed of it"
"Wouldn't do anything different"
"We meant only good"
"Taking part in the demonstration."

"THEY"
Remember him only
As an enemy of their system

"THEY"
Took his body
But not his spirit

Rosie's spirit lives on
Until the last person
Who knew him is dead
We respected him.
We know what he stood up and fought for

Rosie loved to travel
He is on another trip
With friends who went before

- David WALKER
- Nat TURNER
- Paul BOGLE
- Marcus GARVEY
- Patrice LUMUMBA
- Bobby SEALS
- Steve BIKO
- Martin Luther KING
- MALCOLM X
- Walter RODNEY
- Bob MARLEY
- Beverly JONES
- Guy HAREWOOD
- Brian JEFFERS
- The CHILDREN of SOWETO
- Maurice BISHOP

TRAVEL IN PEACE, ROSIE.

2000 DRAMA

Parents decided to reunite
Being apart for years
Being married for years
Separated after two children

Children taken to North America
By their mother
Daughter is fifteen
The son is now ten.
In no time

After being apart
Children are attached to father.
Spending their time together.
Telling old-time stories,

Looking at pictures and movies.
Also listening to music
Becoming very close.

Mother planned trip
Visiting Europe
Father didn't want to go.

Involved with woman
He had for nine years.
Didn't want to leave her
As his wife did.

Day arrives for the trip
Mother
Daughter
Son

Rushing for the boat.
Father and male friend
Assisting them for the trip

On a boat filled with travelers.
Horn sounding as they leave
Bridge and ropes removed.
Boat slowly leaving the harbor.

Father and friend are on board.
Decide to jump off the bow.
They make it safely ashore.
Son also wants to leave.

Doesn't want to leave his father's side
A drama starts
Between mother,
Daughter
And son.

Mother and daughter try
To keep son on board.
Passengers trying to help
Father on land shouting,
Stay on the boat.

Son on boat shouting
Don't want to leave you.
Mother and son
Involved in drama.

Father and friend in drama
Drama in the water 2
A whale.
Unusual.

Yes, unusual,
Large whale in salt water
Moving toward the boat.

Small boat taking passengers
Toward the ship sitting midstream.
Passengers in the small boat
Screaming with fear.

Friends and relatives on shore
In horror by the sight
Father shocked.

Father tells his friend
Going to kill the whale.
Father gets in a small boat
Heading out for the kill.

Other men following
In hot pursuit
Father gets close
Whale biting the boat.

He aims and fires
Hitting the whale's head.
Other men, helping
The water turns red.

Whale starts moving
Like a top
Disrupting all around.
Passengers in the boat
Getting wet to the bone.

All eyes on the men
Killing the whale.
New drama in sight
Between mother,
Daughter
And son.

No help this time
Passengers filled with fear
Not for mother and boy child
All worried making it alive

Son jumps in father's boat.
Hold your brain waves!
Awaking out of the dream.

2000 POSITIVE-NEGATIVE FORCES

Positive force
Food for the mind
Positive state of mind

Words like
Don't
Shouldn't
Must not be used.

2001 HAS THE CHANGE REALLY COME?

Life is a change.
Change is a part of life's cycle.

Life keeps changing
Also the seasons

From hot to cold.
From cold to hot

From season to season
Change creates nature and life.

Change brings a soul into being.

Touches us like a warm wind.

Like a face-to-face meeting
Moving into a happy zone.

Is it really?

Is there control over change?

Change advances.
So does the mind

Some can't accept change
Don't know why

There is fun and laughter.
When the searching is over

Time is essence
In creation and being united

Cosmic forces bring change.
Positive vibes move us.
But will they sustain love?

Try understanding oneness.
Searching for togetherness.

Can I find it?

Must leave the past.

Looking for progress.

Positive thoughts
Positive experiences.

Changes started with one and one.
Then it developed into three.
Now it is back to one human.
So let it be.

2001 I AND I

Not complaining.
Not feeling insecure.
Getting older.

Love to know.
Is there someone around
Around to build a future?

What is needed at this stage of life?
Can I love any female I meet?
Have learnt to love self.

The big question
Do women trust men?
Gotten over the fear

Need a loving relationship.
According to the good book.
Man and woman.
Unite
And become one.

Meet a loving woman this time.
Will tell her I am ready for love

Love building a relationship.
Aware of each other's trials
Experience these trials

Problems
How are they solved?
Dead don't encounter trials.

According to a writer,
Everything needs a negative-positive.
Also in a female-male relationship
Balance
Harmony
Consciousness.

Balance has to be perfect,
Experiences are necessary.
No balance means life of unbalance.

Stay within a positive relationship
Or lose touch with life's practical side
You float off in a spiritual mist.

Someone stated,
"Everyone can be nice to others"
But nothing gets done about it.

A serious negative imbalance
Manifests into extreme negative behavior,
- Anger,
- Aggression,
- Conflict

Control and dominance produce
- Pain,
- Fear and
- Suffering in all its forms.

2001 SOME OF THE PROBLEMS IN RELATIONSHIPS

Questions are important in relationships
Ignored at the beginning of the love affair.
When they do arise, total structure falls apart.

What are the roles in relationships?
Which identity should a child maintain?
Child born of African and European

Where are the two lovers from?
Where are they going in this world?
Who has the last word in a discussion?

Female or male?
Should there be space for disappointment?
What time frame is enough for observation?

Should the children get too close to a lover?
Should lovers fight for control over each other?
Why does one person struggle for control of the other?

Should the love for children be shared with a lover?
Is paying the bills a joint venture?
Whose responsibility is it paying bills?

When does hate and anger develop?
Does lack of love and togetherness bring it on?
What gives rise to distrust and insecurities?

Why do woman or man investigate each other?
Should making the most money give one control?
Why?

Can't we live in love, peace and harmony?
You are you and I am I.
Nothing can change that.

Experiences are a part of lives.
Try investing in a relationship.
Will be repaid with love, honesty and trust.

Developing into a fruitful affair with unity
Woman/man should be proactive and not reactive.
THE ENTIRE UNIVERSE IS CREATED WITH LOVE, BY LOVE, AND IN LOVE.

2001 WOMAN, GIVER OF LIFE

Woman is the goddess.
Woman is the creator.
Woman is the queen.

Woman gives us love.
Woman makes us
Woman gives us life

Woman cares and protects us.
Women gave the first lesson in life.
Women gave us our first hug.

Women help us make the first step
Woman must be honored and respected.
Woman must receive love and not hate.

Unite and continue to praise our women.

2001 SURPRISE IN EMERGE WITH MOTHER AND SICK CHILD

Father out de house all night
Catchin' thin' in flight.
Mother an sick child
Rushin' de emerge at night.
NO SURPRISE.

Mother an sick child
Rushing in de emerge door with plight.
Security takin' no time
Helpin' like flies in flight.
SURPRISE!

Security movin'
Wheelchair brought in time.
Tryin' to get a handle
Watchin' Mother cross-eyed.
NO SURPRISE.

Inside emerge, note sayin',
"Take a number an wait in de line."
Or stay tight as Caribbean people say.
Mothers an their sick standin'
In de line waitin' on time.
NO SURPRISE.

Immigrant mothers come together,
Talkin' about their child in no time.
Helpin' each other in quick time.
NO SURPRISE.

The mothers makin' a change,
Talkin' emerges bad system dis time.
Immigrant mothers within hours
Joinin' together in search of rights.
NO SURPRISE.

Stone-face woman nurses,
Lookin' like workin' hard on mothers' time.
Can't even talk nice to dem,
Behind de wall an glass.
NO SURPRISE.

Dem nurses look
Like STIFFS on ice with no smile.
There is an invisible wall
For some time.
NO SURPRISE.

Between mothers' sick children
An emerge staff at large.
Immigrant mothers keepin' check
For dem non-immigrant mothers.
Who playin' dem na see de invisible line inside.
NO SURPRISE.

"NEXT," Thunder-like voice
Sounds inside.
Dem mothers keepin' dem eyes
On the line fo wan long time.
Knows which one needs help inside.
NO SURPRISE.

Cold an stone-face, medical worker
Waitin' inside.
Playin' de game all de time.
Immigrant mothers sittin' outside
Watchin' an knows de game playin' inside.
NO SURPRISE.

Another sound comes from inside,
"Have your children's information ready in time."
Mothers an sick children know from outside
They will be out of de line in no time.
NO SURPRISE.

Woman medical work asks wan Mother inside,
"What is wrong with de child dis time?"
It's like a medical court start inside,
Ruled by de cold-face woman judge inside.
NO SURPRISE.

De cold-face woman worker
Retakes de child's information
They already have stored inside.
She lookin' for wan WHITE LIE
De mother never told any time.
NO SURPRISE.

In no time,
Her eyes are off de computer
On de sick child
Lookin' for no-information,
Did de mother abuse de child?
NO SURPRISE.

No bruises, no cuts
No blood outside de sick child.
Still lookin' SURPRISE,
Wonderin' if de mother hit she child.
NO SURPRISE.

Losin' time,
Not findin' how sick is de child
Needin' help from de doctor inside.
De non-medical judge
Wastin' time outside
Decidin' which doctor fo de sick child
When the sick child goes further inside.
SURPRISE!

Now further inside,
De sick child waits on de doctor,
Takin' she sweet time.
Female doctor arrives on her time,
No information on de sick child by she side.
SURPRISE!

Askin' questions of de sick child,
Ignorin' de mother at bedside.
Mother answers before de sick child,
Showin' she is not ignored for any time.
SURPRISE!

Mother an child, facin' another trial inside
Not findin' a crime committed on de child
Doctor tries to make de mother an sick child
Feel guilty for seekin' help dis time.
SURPRISE!

Mother an not her sick child rejected
Woman doctor giving negative vibes.
Woman doctor asks again for information
De sick child's information, she left behind.
SURPRISE!

Woman doctor after wantin' left surprised
Hoping for wan surprise from de sick child.
Then find out de sick is really de mother's child.
All den doin' is wastin' time on de sick child
SURPRISE!

De female medical specialist
Next arrives in on time.
In no change of style,
Usin' de same pretext
In different way one more time.
SURPRISE!

De female medical specialist
Askin' for de sick child medical file,
Then said she didn't know it was outside.
After de sick child's mother
Gave her wan watch with strong eyes.
SURPRISE!

She leaves de mother an sick child
Doctor returns around de same time
Pretendin' she doin' somethin' new
Re-doin' de same thin'
De woman specialist did before.
SURPRISE!

De sick child's mother tells de doctor
It was done just wan short while ago.
But de doctor goes on still for a time
Payin' de child's mother no mind.
SURPRISE!

De medical woman doctor
Refuses lookin' de sick child's mother
In her eyes for some time
Findin' out de sick child is de same child
She sees there all de time.
SURPRISE!

Sufferin' from de same complain
Each time they arrive.
Refusin' de information given
From de sick child's mother since they arrive.
NO SURPRISE.

Bad blood develops
Between de sick child's mother
An de woman medical doctor in time.
Before de woman doctor gives medical help
To de immigrant woman's sick child.
SURPRISE!

For de repeated time
De sick child's mother had to protest.
De woman doctor couldn't even inject
De sick child without a fight
SURPRISE!

De sick child's mother
Had to help de woman doctor in no time
So her sick child could ease de pains
Given reluctantly by medical staff.
SURPRISE!

That is how de long night was spent
Between de sick child, de mother
And de medical so-called help.
SURPRISE!

2001 THE FIRST TIME I SAW YOU

The first time I saw your face
Fear entered my body and mind
Should I?
I did not know why.

The next time I saw your face
You captured my loving heart
But not my thoughts
Took time to understand why.

Now my thoughts are forced
Forced to daily think of you.
Thoughts that are haunting
I do not know why.

Now my mind is invaded
Invaded with love for you
But is it mine?
Really do not know why

You have enslaved my body
But my thoughts remain mine.
Why can't I accept yours?
Do you have a hidden agenda?
Agenda for my body and mind

Making me accept your strange love.
Strange love not to be shared with me
Even your thoughts were not yours.
Have found self-love so I can be me.

Stop! Stop! Stop!
Please get out of my head
Stop being in my dream
You have not captured me.
I know and understand why.

No more of your stolen ideology.
My search has given rise to freedom
And understanding.
I know and really understand me.

2001 I AM A HUMAN 2

I am human 2.
Born of a mother 2.
Cared for by a mother 2.
Loved by a father 2.

I am human 2.
Created just as you 2.
Born just as you 2.
Breathe just as you 2.

I am human 2.
Have a brain as you 2.
Can think as you 2.
Could smile as you 2.

I am a human 2.
Have feelings as you 2.
Have wants as you 2.
Have a desire to love as you 2.

I am a human 2.
I can see the sun as you 2.
I can touch a flower as you 2.
I can feel the soft drops of the rain as you 2.

I am human 2.
Three stages of life we must pass 2.
Death is a voyage we must take 2.
Why can't we live in oneness 2?

I am human 2.
Can you see me 2?
Can you hear me 2?
Can you find me 2?

2001 WHY CALL ME SELFISH

Look around you.
Is nature selfish?
What would you say?

If you recognize nature is selfish
We are also a product of nature
Then we are also selfish.

We are also selfish beings
Look again at nature.
One seed gives life to a tree.

A seed produces more than one fruit
From the seeds when planted come trees
Would it amaze you?
We call it strange.

The cycle of life ends with death
Nature creates woman and man.
Then woman and man create
1 egg + 1 sperm = 1 child.

The process can be called selfish.
Look again at the cycle of life.
Woman can create many children
Would you say she is selfish?

Some are astonished.
Surprise is used and not strange.
Some cry and some are shocked.
Others might call it selfishness.

Two eggs united.
Creating a Life.
Then,
Child (teenage),
Adult (middle and old age)
And Death.
So is not that selfishness?

Think.
Do you still call me selfish?
Think.

2001 YOU DID NOT CREATE ME

You did not create me.
Why try to control?

You did not feed me as a child.
Why try to take my food away?

If you do not know me now
You would never know me.

Why not take time to know me?
Try to understand me some

You do not listen to me.
Nor hear my message

If you do not love yourself
You can't share love with me

2003 BLACK WOMAN AND MAN

What is the reason or reasons?
There is no unity and love
Between Black women and men

Woman and man cannot get along
Did it begin during slavery or after?
No, the system was designed that way.

Using one person against the other.
Women fighting against men
Men fighting men for woman

Children against parents
Was it the whipping in slavery?
The whippings of women

The whippings of children
The after-effects of slavery
Woman's abdomen cut open
In childbirth and her child removed.

Left to die without objecting or fighting.
Her child taken by the slave owner.
Child taken out from her womb

In front of the man/husband unable to help
He could not or would have been killed.
Has this anger been passed down in the genes?

Is it the uncertain life in the world?
Is it the fear of living in a controlled world?
Is it an inability of sharing loving?

Has it given rise to continual anger?
Is it hate between woman and man?
They do not understand each other

Or know the other.
Men should be proactive
Not reactive
REAL LOVE NEEDS NO PREPARATIONS.

2003 ALTERED STATE (A Caribbean Perspective)

Were guns and shooting in our blood?
Were guns a part of the Black society?

Was killing a part of Black society?
Did we kill each other by gun?

Were we exposed to use the gun?
Did we grow up with guns in our homes?

No, it was pushed on us.
In Hollywood/MGM movies

Hollywood taught and it was idealized
Do we make and sell guns in our society?
Made and brought in by the ruling class

Who sold the guns and made money?
How did the guns get into our society?
Brought in by the seller and used on us

The gun became their equalizers.
Can we not live in an altered state?
No, it is part of the controlled plan.

Planned by the ruling class.
Can the ruling class stop the altered state?
No, it is how they maintain control over us.

Could the masses change the system?
They are not in control of the altered state.
The equalizer is a population control tool.

The rulers engage in population control
Population control in their wars
Destroying non-white societies.
Drug has become an equalizer too.

Who is responsible for the drugs in North America?
We are totally in a society that is a controlled state.
We are shooting up on drugs without care.
We are living like zombies in their societies.
We are living in their altered state directed by them.
We have to return to African-centric thoughts.

2003 MY TRIP TO JAMAICA

Areas with massive developed hills
High and low when driving by.

Creating sculpture forms in the sky.
O what a perfect sight from afar.

Hills far and wide with virgin greens

Lay like carpets in front of the blue sky.
Along the Caribbean sunny sky

O what an artistic expression in sight.

Land with swift moving water.
From high above to lands below
Running uncontrollable as it sees
As rain falls from dark skies above

O what an amazing creator's sight.
Land of unstoppable running water
Taking on a mind and force of its own.
Moving rapidly and gracefully along

From mountaintops high above.
O what a master of nature in sight.
Land with various mountain shapes
Along country winding roads.

Running wildly along.
Along nature's massive art

O what an unusual progression of sight.
Land with many sloping paths

And narrow constructed roads.
Moves around hidden turns
From enormous heights to below
O what a nerve-wracking drive

Making sharp turns as you drive
Land with these hidden bends
Below hillside trees rooted in rocks
Accompanied by fearless drivers
Aggressive and seen after a horn

Proceeding with speed in the dark.
O what a breathtaking feeling and sight
With heartrending move along the roads
Land with elevated roads rise above water

Elevations from 100 to 600 feet high up
With houses built hidden between trees
Below the roads or high above the hills
O what perfect building fitted in nature.

Do any of us know how?

Note (an afterthought):
Traveling high above.
As motionless dot along the path
Traveling vehicle in haste
Looks the same in sight.
Flash of light
moving with sound.
You hear and see the moves.
Can you see me hidden between the trees?

2003 IN JAMAICA EVERYTHING MOVES

Jamaica high lands sloping
Move upward to the sky
From low plains leading
To extremely high heights

Making downward paths
Toward unusual directions

Unusual scenic sights ahead
Mountains reaching the sky

City roads moving along
Suddenly inland with turns
Creating unusual turns ahead
Running wildly along the land

Moving out, in and around hills
Embracing high mountains in sight
As undivided lovers do when in love
Creating small and winding curves

With no support for protection
On the left as road descends.
Make a bad move any time.
It is down from above the hill
In cars, vans, buses or truck.

Yes, no protective guards on the sides
Earth and stone sliding down the hill
Mash-up when crash to the ground
Very few live after the fall from above

Water moving uncontrollable down
Like the roadways under its path
As it rains from the sky high above
Moving forceful without care below
Moving from heights far above land

Rushing hard below
In surrounding lands
Below and beyond its start
In haste and uncontrollable
Rushing below in speed

Unstoppable on its course
Speeding along the slopes
Taking everything for a ride.
Changing color as it moves

Merging with earth below.
In deep sculptural passages
Creating groves with force.
Making sharp turns traveling down

Drivers like water moving along roads.
Moving up and down winding roads.
Fearless and hurriedly in no time
Making money for their daily lives

Drivers in cars and trucks
Competing for small spaces.

Along steep and winding roads
Every minute of the day

Sounds of car horns can be heard.
Either for a warning to the unseen
Or a friendly blow when passing on by

2003 AMERICANIZED (Information Overload)

Jamaican government is the same
As any other Caribbean country
Controlled by the IMF and USA

As other foreign countries 2
Plenty of television stations
And radio stations in the place.

Pushing only foreign news 2.
Twenty foreign TV stations on air.
Few local stations for poor 2 watch
Upper class don't look at local news
They are only attracted to foreign shows

Most thinking foreign is true 2.
A war of words is daily fought 2

Between the rich and poor 2
Rich maintain their richness
And the poor remain poor 2.

Upper class always making jokes
About the political system
And the poor people 2
The poor hustling in vain to make life 2
While the rich living life in comfort 2

Plenty small streets, big cars and trucks
And plenty speed 2 that kill many 2
Everyone is fighting for what they can take
Fighting for the same cause, the US dollar 2.

Tourists are their prey

They are easy to spot
There is still one love 2

In all its people's hearts 2

2003 SMILE

You don't smile
When we are together
It makes me feel invisible

Should there be a reason to smile?
Do you feel fine around me?
Why was I invited on this trip?

What is your problem with me?
An attempt was made to join you.
What more do you want me to do?

Then just leave me alone.
Let me enjoy this trip
Working things out in my head.

Can't we enjoy this trip?

2003 INSECURITY IS KNOCKING

Sleep tight.
Kiss, and kiss
Need another kiss
Before I sleep.

Is the kiss for security?
No, just need another kiss
No, don't feel like kissing
Why can't I get another kiss?

She got mad.
Left the room.
Returned three hours later
Still mad

You asked for the truth.
But you cannot handle it.

2003 I AM IN TOTAL SHOCK

Never expected to experience shock.
Culture shock in the Caribbean Island
Culture shock in Jamaica not my home
Culture shock was really a shock
You could call me naïve but I don't care.
Irie.

Jamaica
Was the training ground
For newly arrived slaves
Brought to the (West Indies) Caribbean
From Africa against their will in boats
Under the then British control system.
You could call me naïve but I don't care.
Irie.

Suppressive system keeping people in line
Trained slaves (house niggers and field slaves)
Became rebellious
Shipped to other areas in the Caribbean.
You could call me naïve but I don't care.
Irie.

Slaves that refused British training
Rebelled and escaped into the hills
Revolted against their ruling system
That was suppressive and inhumane
You could call me naïve but I don't care.
Irie.

To name a few who revolted,
- The Maroons,
- Paul Bogle,
- Marcus Garvey and
- Bob Marley.

You could call me naïve but I don't care.
Irie.

People keep talking about slavery
And what the white man did.
Being suppressed by the man
Who claims it is not his fault
But fault of his forefathers.
You could call me naïve but I don't care.
Irie.

Black community divided after 1962.
Manley took over and people ran out.
Rich and educated left the country fast
Opposing the changes in the land.
Working class supporting government
Pushing African-centric views around
You could call me naïve but I don't care.
Irie.

Jamaica is a multicultural society
Filled with races of different lands
- Africans
- Germans
- Jews
- Russians
- Brits

- Syrians
- Indians
- Spanish
- Chinese
- Cubans
- Australians

Living with locals
Was totally surprised
Foreigners staying put
The rich move together
Also support each other.
You could call me naïve but I don't care.
Irie.

Some local men marry foreign women
Some started businesses to make money
Married men continue outside relationships.
Foreign wives in the yard raising children
Educated local women marry foreign men
Claiming local men have nuff women around
You could call me naïve but I don't care.
Irie.

Upper class control the lives of the poor
"Man to man is so unjust
You don't know who to trust." Bob Marley.
You could call me naïve but I don't care.
Irie.

The poor people trying hard
Divided by political system
Failed by their government
Living under the class system
Rulers keeping people suppressed
You could call me naïve but I don't care.
Irie.

2004 THE LOVE BUG

You cannot fix
What you don't want to face.
Failure to choose
Is fear of keeping the old
We choose not to learn.

How can I love you?
Could you state how?
Would it be no love?
Would it be a hard job?

Trying hard to know
Can you be given love?
Open up and see love

Is there any freedom
For woman or man?
Bad love is rushed
Love times takes years.

Life is filled with the past
Then joined by a future
Love sharing love to you
Honest and respectful affair

Developing into lasting love
Not broken as it grows
Love in process, cannot be stopped.

Could growth be prevented in unity?
Could attention stop its progress?
Love affair has rules and order.
Either we accept it or it dies.
Was your love really for me?

2004 BROKEN CARIBBEAN ENGLISH

Oman an man na know what dem want in life.
Oman an man get in verbal fights in dem house
She call de police fo put him out de family house

Oman hold Bible in dem hand fo keep de man out
Him get put out de house an can't return fo clothes.
Getting tough fo oman an man living in foreign now

Couples workin' from mornin' 'til night na know each other
Get tie up in de system an forget bout makin' life an love
Losin' dem culture an forget how
dem live in dem country
Everythin' oman an man see pon TV
dem a copy fo true

Oman nor man na a mek home no more in foreign land
Breakin up mek dem children go astray fo sure
Oman an man livin' together now ave nuff problems
Narth Merica a mek nuff oman an man ave it ard fo live

Dem fighting over what is oman an man work in
de home.
Oman an man na got independent like in de Caribbean
Man ave no more power cause foreign is wan oman world
Omen dem get more rights under de new foreign system.

Oman dem
talk tough cause dem now ave rights over de man
Now dem think
dem know it all but is wan foreign trap fo true
TV watchin' all day is part of de plan an
brainwashing fo we
Oman sa dem na lov man de same an na
givin' up dem power

Fool man dem sa dem love dem an still lookin' fo control more
Man know dem
can hardly angle one an na learn nothin' yet.
Man still tryin' fo make it wid nuff oman dem afta dem can't.
Oman dem sa dem na know wa dem man dem want in life

Men sa dat de oman dem na even know wat dem want too.
Hope de day come when all dem know what dem wants fo true.
Dem have fo mek up dem mine if dem want each other or not.
Oman must member dat man is part from oman too.

Man lef like boat wid out paddle pun trouble wata.
Oman na know if dem can andle man no more.
Some oman pass thirty sa dem stop havin' sex.
Dis habit a mek man 'eart a hurt bad bad bad.

Dem oman only keep man fo wan short time now
An tell man dat thin' change an na want fa see dem
When hard time come an reality hit dem, dem can tek it.
Oman gon get trouble cause dem really mix up, mix up.
In de system mek by Whitey causin' division in de camp
Oman na even happy in dem own ouse when dem alone.
Always out buyin' nuff thin' fo mek dem happy in
de ouse.

Me think dem got fo look
inside dem self an den come outside.
Man also got fo love dem self first before dem can love
wan other
Man must member dat dem is wan part of oman too.
Man dem must be forget.

2004 WAN TRIP PUN DE BUS IN TORONTO

Wan day me bin a travel pun de Ossington bus.
Me friend get into a little trouble in de bus

Yo see him come to Canada wid bit-ta-ness in him mind.
Wid what him read bout how Narth Merica treat immigrants

Him was like turkey wid nuff passion
Hate tak over him soul fo sure

Anyway him bin a go pun da bus.
Wan white man a come off de same time.

Push wan Indian Caribbean gal out de way.
Den tel she fo move she nigger self out de way.

Him was surprise at de man.
Where him com from, dem say.

Dat man dress in suit a good man.
Dis one was no good wan.

Him views change afta him see wha de suit man do.
All him learn before he come, him put unda him foot.

Dis time a white man pass him an mash he foot.
De same foot me friend bin hurt at him work place.

Him bawl out, O God, an at de same time him hit de man.
De man fall pun de ground in he suit an it get mess up.

As the man get up him go tell de bus driver.
De white driver get up and walk to the back of the bus.

Call out to me friend fo came
But him na pay him no mind.

Him lef de bus an walk out de station fo him ouse.
Him stay about one hour an leave again fo tak de bus.

As him a go back to de station
Him see bout six police outside de subway.

De police walkin' round de subway station lookin'.
Me friend stand up in front one of de police car.

And him askin' one of de police, a wha appen.
De police say dat dem a look fo a man

Dat assault wan white man pon de bus.
De police ma know him a de person dem a look fa.
He left an pass de rest of police too an dem na know a he.

2004 DE PLACE ME FUS WOK IN NART MERICA

Me had fo tak de King Street car.
Fo go to wuk three to eleven shift.
Day, afternoon an night
Cause me a do shift work.

Dis was me third job me had
De place was wan big weldin' factree.
An in de place all man a do piece wuk.
Weldin' nuff pieces a metal together makin' parts.
Fo mak extra money on me biweekly pay cheque.

Me had fo wuk like wan mad dog on de shift nonstop.
Me had one hour lunch an two fifteen minutes a shift.
Doin' piece wuk me ave fo do seven hours on de job.

Fo mak de day pay an keep de wuk.
De wuk place full of nuff white foreman.
Walkin round de wuk site
Watch if me a do me wuk.

Dem foreman was like slave driver.
Eight hours an five days' wan week.
Dem also change shift round de clock.

When me change shift me never feel right.
Me body all mix up an me tun wan robot.

Yo enter de wok place yo ave fo punch timecard.
When yo lef yo ave fo punch out so yo pay cheque okay.
If me miss de punch card wan shift dem sa yo na wok.
An yo get short pay from de system leaving yo hungry.

Before me forget me gat fo tell yo dis
Wha mak me a tel de story an lef de wuk
Me betta tell yo one time an not get carried away
Wid de Narth Merican system.

Wan day early spring me bin a weld in de shop.
De place hot hot wid dem machine givin' hot air.
De hot air mek me body give off water like waterfall.

De place outside bin a change from very cold to warm.
An me bin a feel like in hell wid de heat in de wuk place.
So me take it pun me self fo open up de door fo get air.

Cool breeze dat me can get some ease from de heat.
Me go back fo wuk pun de job an weld some more.
Me stop wuk again an find de place dark, dark, dark.

Before me tak me weldin' shield off na walk to de door.
De shield com off me see somebody close de door again.
So me go open de door again an me feel wan hand pun me.

De hand touch me an it also push me out of de way.
Was de foreman an me chuck him back an him fall
Him fall to de ground an me get fired from de job.

2004 WHY IT TOOK SO LONG?
I Must Get Out of the Cold

It really take long fo me to realize
So long to realize I should not be here
In this strange, cold and foreign land

No — it was always dormant and quiet.
Suppressed in my attempts to achieve
Afraid to move because no money.

Out of a strange, cold and foreign land
Have not gotten accustomed to and will never
Living suppressed since Nov. 1971 and hooked

Hooked like a fish on a hook and not free
In a fantasy dream wanting to be freed
Eating genetic engineered bad foods

Promoted as great food to eat for nourishment
It is killing my body and soul for sure
Killing my body and soul making me sick

Sickly and real unsure that I cannot leave
Today I ask myself some hard questions
That're going around in my confused head

Hard to get answered outside if asked
Why did I come and why have I stayed so long?
How long can I really stay in this place?

The repeated struggles that never stop
Have become real hell and stressful too
I can't leave this uncomfortable state

This cold place and its cold people. Cold!
The ground filled with snow and freezing rain.
Public transportation so far not in sight

Passengers at the bus stop cold and in anger
Crying, "Where is the dam bus?"
Standing here for two, three hours or more

Everything moving on wheels or feet on the road
Sliding and slipping as I stand waiting and freezing
Really how much more can I take of this cold?

Somehow I have now missed the Caribbean
Hot sun and warm people with smiling faces.
That loving cultural place of my place of birth

Grew up in it and I long to be a part of it again
I am not growing accustomed to this cold place
No matter how long I try staying in the cold

Will the strength ever come from within?
Really don't know why I came in the first place
What made me listen to the salesperson who did the sale?

Poisoned idea filled with false hopes and no economic stability
Who or what placed me in this altered state of mind?
The sale is now final and accepted by me

Foreign trainers (con artist) educator and news reporter.
Spreading their foreign values that are not mine and real.
Suppressing my culture that has a historical track record

Proven and historical track record of African cultural values
Left behind, especially by the young people in most cases
Some adults not hanging on to the "new market culture."

Keeping the old track record (not written but spoken by our past Elders)
The foreign trainers willfully never taught it so it must die.

Also neglected or rejected by their dominant sector

Exchanged for a colonial political system, not built on love
Filled with fighting wars, individualistic wants and self-desires.
A system of false hopes built on self-pleasures and control.

You/yours is mine, take more, no love for self or others,
Every day competitions filled with hate, war and killings.
A belief system built on divide, conquest and rule.
Divide, acquire and rule every other culture foreign.
Old cultural values no longer understood in the society.
Moving toward a new world order that is foreign and unstable.
Developing within the new world system of division and no unity
Race against race, religion against religion
Woman and man of every culture against each other,

Children and parents against each other
Children against each other and themselves
Unemployment, poverty and beggars rising

An implemented plan by the dominant sector
Maintaining their continual economic stability
Staying in power over other cultures around the world.

They did it before and are doing it again (today).
The game is the same; only the players have changed.
Old values become inferior to their new society.

Pushing their cultural values within suppressing nations
Marginalized and ghettoized (e.g., Slavery, Africa, Caribbean,
India, Cuba, Iran, Iraq, Haiti, Afghanistan and Palestine —
to name a few).

2004 CHANGES BEFORE ME EYES

In 1996 me an me family move
To wan place pun Bathurst Street.
Me live in de place for few years.
Move cause de place get small.

More family come fo live wid me.
So me had fo move again fo sure.
Me had stop drive pass de old place.
Den me pass an see wan sign all got fo move.

De owner sell to another developer.

Dem a put up high-rise apartment.

Giving de old resident first chance fo buy.
De oman me bin a live wid na want fo buy.

Look how we na got sense.
Do not know if we gon ever
Look how things change fast.
Change is de only permanent ting.

2005 HIGHEST ACHIEVEMENTS (Through Nature)

It is a natural process
Nature recycles itself.
Repeating a rebirth for life
Resurrection.

Like the rose at springtime,
Filled with new life after winter.
Nature's revitalizing process.
Plants hibernate during winter

Revitalize themselves at birth.
Don't complain about the process.
Don't complain about harsh elements
Have you ever seen a rose complain?

Humans complain about the stages of life.
Even if it is good or bad
Enduring change is part of our being.
Remember,

Change is a process we have to go through.
So accept change when confronted by it.
Experience teaches wisdom, yet some fail to learn.
The stages are a resurrection process in the path of life.

Some of us are granted chances to repair mistakes.
Few are fortunate to recognize this process of change.
Many don't even receive a call to recycle natural love.
To recycle love is to forgive and not be revengeful.

A process of growing up and understanding human desires.
Granted chances mean giving moral support to others.
Moral support while reaching out toward others.
Reaching out and projecting care for the other.

A chance is not given for exercises of one's hate and anger.
Should be recognized as one of the highest stages in life
Traveling through the process of sharing one's love is unique.
Through attaining self-love, one can give unique free love.

Learning and understanding to give freely and receive freely.
It is better to give love than to receive it because life is short.

We all make mistakes but only a few learn from them.
The only problem is most of us do not admit to them.
It is true we should gain wisdom from our experience.
So why do we repeatedly play mind-games and get the same results?

Accept those with love and be reasonable; it's a part of growing up.
Growing up is a chance to love one more time and accept change.
Accept the change and overcome the negative of the past.
"Do not take bread from their mouths if you cannot give biscuits."

Be supportive in endeavors that make them happy.
Be a listener with understanding and with love.
Talk more with your inner mind and not with an evil tongue.
"Never take anything from a person unless you can replace it."

Live not for you but with the understanding of the other person.
Let peace live within you and wisdom be your guide.
Guide your thoughts by connecting with love and not war.
"Live the life you are living and love the life you live."

Given another chance is a rebirth/resurrection.
Given a second chance is to be sincere toward the other.
Given another chance is being patient with the other.
Giving another chance is not doing what you did in the past.

2005 GETTING OVER A WRONG DONE TO YOU

Getting over a relationship
Don't get even
With the person
Who did you wrong.
You forgive and don't get even
With that person,

You haven't gotten over that problem.
In continuing to beat the hell
Out of that person
You have not got over the wrong.

Getting over a broken relationship
Is tough.
Don't be hard on the next person.
Do not open a new relationship
Before closing the other door.

It is not easy to sometimes
Say no out of fear.
Why not take the hard road?
And say yes.
No matter what is said
Forgive each other please.

Refusing to forgive that person
Your power would be taken away.
When you are hurt
In a broken relationship
Do not let the other person
Keep their power over you.

2005 IDEAS DEVELOPED OVER THE YEARS

Don't be surprised
Have written thoughts
Developed over the years.
A part of life's development.
Better future.

Believe in building a future.
With a loving female
Who understands.
Believe that in this world
Repeated struggle is a part.

It does not pay to be upset
Or make others upset.
Woman is the boss in any relationship.
Most men might be upset
At the statement but it is true.

Think about it.
If we (men) are from women (mothers)
Then we must respect and love them.
Women are the captains of their ships.
Fathers and children are the followers.
We join the ship with the captain.

Traveling the international highway of life.
Men think that they start and control
A relationship with woman
But it is the other way around.
It is the woman who controls.
(See the movie *LOVE JONES*).

2006 JUSTIFY

You don't have to justify your return to love.
You don't have to justify sharing your love.
You don't have to justify because you don't.

I don't have to justify your return to love.
I don't have to justify sharing your love.
I don't have to justify because I don't.

Are we not taught to share our love?
Are we not taught to love our neighbors?
Are we not taught it is better to love than to hate?

It is better to cross the path from hate to love.
It is a freedom that some humans enjoy. So make it.
The other freedom is making the choice for self.

Why should there be any justification because we are in love?
Why should there be any justification because of a reunion?
Why should there be any justification between two adults?

2007 ARE WE PREPARED FOR THIS LIFE?

Why do we think life will give us everything?
It cannot.

It is built on a system of repeated struggle
From the time of birth to our death.
It is a developmental experience filled with
– Good and evil,
– Right and wrong,
– False expectations with no internal positive values,
– The haves and the have-nots within a class system,
– Lack of internal visualizing and self-growth,
– Built on values of capitalism

2011 YO WANT DE TRUTH BUT YO CAN'T HANDLE IT

Afta me walk round
Like if me sleep walkin.'
Fo some time

Me belly na stop hurting.'
Wid tears in me eye
An me want fa ball out.

Cause me belly hurtin'
From de place dat really change.
It far from what me lef.

An know dat me own people
Now total stranger to me.
Cause me now stranger to dem too.

An dem ave no fate in one nada.
Nor respect.
No more trust.

No order in de place too.
Everybody
Want wan small piece.

An now everythin' yo want.
Yo got fo pass wan handout.
Wid de right hand too.

- Duns-eye.
- Malalee.
- Bread.

- Dustie.
- Chit-na.
- An greens fo pay

Government service now.
Dat was free in de past.
Me really "bitter-bitter" fo so.

An me feel de taste
In my mouth now fo true.
Me really got fo keep

Me past in me now.
An na bring it out again
Fo look like me mad

Me got fo put it
In me memory
But all de wrong dem.

Still keep knockin' me out
Inside me brain.
Dem government buildin'

From long-long time
Look de same an no repair.
Dem European buildin'

So damn strong.
An got nuff info
Dem keepin' inside.

Dat na burn down yet.
Only de one
Dem can destroy easy.

Dem destroy some already
Wid nuff fire.
Break down de one dem can.

Put up new one in dem spot.
Dem let Christian churches
Burn down too.

An de one dem lef fo stay
A rotten dem fall down.
Dem even mak sale

Fo some a dem in GT
To foreign owners dem.
It is wan shame

How nuff foreigner
Now own land in de place.
An buyin' up all dem old

Historical buildin' in de place.
An de rulers dem
Na care bout we past.

Is it dat time change in de place?
Or dem really change de place
Fo dem own new likin, now?

De place full wid foreigners
Takin' over so easy.
Handin' money to ministers

So dem can own wid no fight.
Leadin' group got nuff money
More dan other group.

An foreign gettin' power
Handed to dem too easy.
Plus, what dem come wid.

Mekin' thin' easy fo dem
Tek what dem want.
De other group come

Wid no money.
But mek money sellin'
Booze an dry food.

What people want?
An now break ground
Buildin' life fo stay.

Startin' fo buy
What dem want wid no fear.
Nobody standin' in dem way.

Dem tekin' de people small piece
An givin' dem what dem needs
Fo survive in de place.

Dem really tekin over de place.
Street by street.
Startin' from de west to de east.

Start wid Robb an Regent Street.
Dat full wid foreigners sellin'
Wha Guyanese want cheap.

Wid all de money dem hide
An get wan free pass in
Wid no problem

An gettin' comfortable
Wid help from dem in charge.
Wid wan hidden agenda

Helpin' put more
In somebody pocket.
But dat gon start

Wan economic war in de place.
Not by de poor
But de money people dem.

Dem dat had wan chance
Before de foreigners get kick out.
But can't mek more money now.

Dem who ruler an don't care
Foreigner dem fullin' up
De place wid cheap good

Dem keep sellin'
Rippin' off dem own people.
De place so change

Dem got four-story malls
Not far from Water Street
Own by we people too.

All dis happenin'
In front of the money people.
Who always got fo so

An dem losin' power
But still attachin'
De poor in de place fo so.

Wha a worry me
Is dat de poor people
Na mean fo wake up

An learn no more
From de past mistakes.
Still helpin' de rich get more rich

Dem stayin' real poor
All over de place.
An dem even makin' up

False charge.
Lockin' up dem own.
All fo wan small handout

From dem crooks in control
As Judas did Christ in de Holy Bible story
Dem did give we fo read.

Me can't stand it
Me can't take it no more
Cause me belly

Na really stop hurtin' me now
All de time in de place me born.
Yo can't trust yo own now

In dis unjust society
Yo na ave fo trust
Wha me sa is true
Go see de place of yo birth fo true.

2011 A SPACE BETWEEN US

Yes, there is physical space between us
It is large distance.
There is difference between time and distance

Being conscious makes distance looks longer.
Subconsciously time and space seem short/timeless.
There is always space between every created thing on earth.
Physical space is a measured distance of movement between two points.

2011 CARIBBEAN "GIVE ME" PROGRAM

Caribbean "give me" program
Give me dis.
Give me dat.

Not even sa please.
Me want dis.
Me want dat.
Dis is how dem survive.

Give me wan drink of rum.
Give me wan beer.
Give me wan small piece.
Me need dis.

Me need dat.
Is de theme song
Give me wan thousand dollars
Give me more.

Dem don't ask fo food.
Me want some change.
Me want wan piece.
Yo got fo give

Or dem don't stop.
It is just give, give, an give.
An want, want, want.
Don't care if yo got or not.

Stretchin' hands in yo face.
Yo must give.
Not knowin' how yo stand.
Dis is what we turn to now.
Dependin' on others an not on self.
And dem mad mad if dem na get

2012 RESPONSE

January 5, 2012 at 4.00 pm.
Got an email
I read it.
Read it.
And read it.

Filled with mixed emotions.
Am I to cry, laugh or mourn?
I do not know how to react.

2012-01-11 TODAY

Remained in a dream state.
Should I talk about it?
But with whom?

I don't even know to whom.
They might never understand
Why I grieve.

Trying to express thoughts in words.
Suffering inward and can only write.
Getting flashbacks.

Doubts about the unknown future linger
In my body, soul and mind.
Why should I worry?

What is the future?
Am I not a human being 2?
Am I being sentimental?

Towards a family I just met.
And never knew.
I could be affected this way

Yes, I am.
I felt safe and relaxed
In the Caribbean arms

From warmth and love
Few people can understand.
Felt good to be free and expressing

Toward warm-minded Caribbean people.
Sharing a common bond in historical path.

Suffering

After achieving free speech
Education
Artistic expressions

Our culture projected in the world.

2012 MY LIFE

Tired of working.
The night shift
At my age

Thought it was great.
Working while others sleep.
Exposed to a new system.

So I can write my thoughts.
With more control over thoughts.
I am not enjoying the trip.

Looking toward a better future.
But can it get to a better life?
Migrated from my country in the '70s.

Forced to accept any type of employment.
Still working the night shift.
With my life controlled.

Becoming a blue-collar worker.
After receiving higher education.
My standard of life has not improved.

But is it a thought wasted?
Looked for a better job after school.
But it never happened.

And again back where I started.
Employed in nonproductive fields.
Retired and got a surprise.

Started to receive a monthly pension.
Isn't much to live on as food cost is rising.
Rent is $880.00 per month and going up.

Imagine living on a hundred dollars per month.
As the cost of living keeps climbing higher.
After rent is paid.

Forced to return to work.
Under the same controlled system.
Where my time remains controlled.

With no freedom.
Cannot do what I want when I want.
Every move is being controlled.

Can't have a real vacation.
Without being told for what time.
What kind of uniform to wear.

What time I must start.
When I can leave.
When to have lunch.

Control what my wages should be.
The hours I must work.
Arrive at a set time.

God forbid if I get sick.
The first day I would not be paid.
Must get a doctor's note to receive my pay.

The funny thing is

I can only be off for six months.
Given short-term disability as a senior.

Younger worker receives one-year disability.
How can it be right?
Nothing can be done about it.

The controlled system remains in place.
After a certain age old people are not needed.
The workforce accepts younger worker.
Can I enjoy the rest of my life before I DIE?
I am going to make it.

2012 RESPONSIBILITY AT WORK

Left for work at 10:00 p.m.
Thinking what to write today.
Thinking and not worrying.
The rain was falling heavily.

Nothing came to mind.
After my 35-minute ride.
My 8-hour shift started.
It was quiet.

Ideas started entering the mind.
Took over the control office.
Shortly after hell broke loose.
Alarms in the building sounded.

It went through the three stages.
The fire department arrived on the scene.
The phone started ringing.
It was the company who monitored the system.

The panel box lit up like an Xmas tree.
Called the engineer on duty, who did not reply.
An officer was sent to the main monitor room.
And another met the fire officers.

The fire department entered the building.
Met at the main door by an officer.
The officer recorded the number of the engine.
Information given.

There was no fire in the building.
Flood in the kitchen, second floor.
Water flowing (heavy) from the sprinkler,
It developed into a river (two feet of water).

Escaping along a passage.
About 100 feet.
Ran and somehow set the alarm off.
Would you believe?

The engineer could not find the shut-off valve.
It was hidden.
Hidden behind a new wall.
Constructed in the summer.

He had to call his boss.
Took three hours to turn the water off.
Thing got back to normal at 4:00 a.m.
Giving me an idea to write about.

2012 THANK GOD IT IS FRIDAY

Today is the last of my workweek.
I am happy.
I will have time and freedom.
I am happy.

Doing what I like on my time.
I am happy.
A few days ago I was reading
An email explaining negative thoughts.

What we learn about money.
Not from within my family.
From people on the streets.
Not happy

I heard money:
- Does not grow on trees.
- Is the root of all evil.
- The problem is not money
- But money is the problem.

2012 THOUGHT

Everything needs a positive and a negative
Even surviving in a loving relationship
Between a woman and man in love.

Creating and developing a perfect balance.
Joined positive and negative experiences
With growth and balance.

In the evolution of a love affair
No balance brings extreme problems.
Don't move too far from unity.

Keep the positive polarity alive.
Keep the end results away from a lost.
Keep with the practical side of life.

Create building blocks to stand on
Preventing the relationship from floating away.

2012 TO MY LOVING PARENTS, WHO HAVE PASSED
(On My Birthday)

12:00 AM
I am happy.
My loving parents' spirit
Has remained alive with me
In the world of repeated struggles.

I thank them for surviving
And their teaching
Making it to this point
Their spirit will continue.

Guiding me
Through the unknown place.
Would not be here without them.
Thinking about my loving mother.

The pains she had
From my birth at home.
Do not know why I felt them.
But I did.

The stages of life mean more
As one gets older.
Thanks, Mother and Dad.

2012 ME HOMELAND

B G, GUYANA, G T, DE MUD.
Or de birthplace me born in.
Dat me na know no more.
De place so change.

Dat me lef in wan dream.
Fo three week
Me a ask nuff question.
About de place from me past

An get cold-shoulder.
An suck teeth.
Mek me stop talk
Dem mek me feel stupid.

An stop lookin'
Fo answer in de present.
An forget de long past.
Me go ome an hardly know

Where me da most time.
Me walk round an round
An na know nothin' no more.
De streets got de same names

But de place change.
All buildin' dat me lookin' fa
Na still standin' up no more.
De favorite place

Me use fa hang round.
Na ave no buildin' now.
But lef empty now.
Wid nuff wild grass growin'

Pun de open spot.
De place busy dan in de past.
Wid nuff people an vehicles.
Movin' in wan real hurry.

Fightin' fa de same space
Pun de same road.
All of dem sidewalks
Full wid nuff venda.

Sellin' de same stuff.
Can't understand
Dem hustle fo survival.
An how dem mak money.

Dem streets an pavements
Now break up
Wid nuff potholes.
De sidewalks dem,

Nights an day.
Wid nuff people
Mekin' bed fa sleep.
Me only had fo use me eye.

An keep me mouth
Lock up tight-tight.
Na fo look like wan stupidee
In wan new place.

An lef de past in de past.
But me got fa sa
Dat me really can't tek it.
Me belly full wid nuff pain.

Feelin' sad fa true.
Wid nuff eye-wata
In me eye.
In de place me love

An born dat gone.

2013 COUPLE ON THE TRAIN 10:00 PM

Woman an man standin' on platform.
Woman entered de car lookin' sick
Leanin' she head pun de man
Me start feel sorry for she

Me stay quiet and start listenin'
Then me hear de man say take it easy
Then the woman came alive an say
She need de man fo look for gifts

Gifts fo she father an brother
He start fo ask what kind of sneakers
Black, white or another color
Then she start put on de charm more

He do not even know what is takin' place
She done make it pun he brain and pocket
He agree and she turn more lovin' on he
A White woman and African man

2013 SUNDAY 22 DECEMBER

The abuser makes you feel helpless,
Confused, Emotionless and
Dirty.
They should go to jail.

2013 CARIBBEAN PEOPLE

Leaving their place of birth
Traveling to foreign lands.
Encounter daily struggles
With past and present teachings

Dealing with culture shock
Foreign has a culture without rich values
The new system filled with many values
Projected outward toward them.

Searching for a better life for their children
But children accept the new system
Accepting the new values and not the past
Holding it as true values.

Creating a struggle with their patents.

2013 MOTHER/WIFE

Are important in any family
When that family is together.
The family head is a loving mother

She understands her family.
She keeps the family united.
She knows each one in her family

Teaches and also protects the young.
Advice to the older children is given by directions.
Few men understand mothers

Don't love and treat them with respect.
But they themselves came from a mother.
Great mothers keep the family together.

Have a happy Mother's Day.

2013-19 DECEMBER MANDELA

Mandela (b-1918 and d-2013)
"Man to man so unjust yo doesn't know who fo trust.
Yo best friend could be yo worst enemy and
Yo worst enemy could be yo best friend." HON BOB MARLEY.

A few shocking events occurred over the past years.
At the same time resulted in surprising endings.
Shocking some of us into reality.

Especially those who are older.
Having experienced the hands
Of those that controlled their (our) lives.

Some of these events we never expected
To end as they did.
They were not as in most of the fairy tales

We were taught and brainwashed to accept
Throughout our educational processes
Or created by Hollywood
Projected toward us on the silver screen.

Events which might have caused some of our grandparents
Not to believe were happening either due to their continual fight for freedom
Thinking that by gaining independence meant that it was the end.

To name a few (not in chronological order);
- The American NASA developing of Apollo 11 and its journey to the moon in 1969.
- The building of the Berlin Wall that separated people and its fall in 1989.
- Elected an African-American President -# 44th (Obama in 2000) who continues to be attacked by those who have money, power and prestige.
- Nations that were suppressed by Eurocentric ideas (like the Haiti revolution between 1791-1804 led by Toussaint L'Ouverture, who was killed fighting for freedom) fought against the ruling class (who refused to give in) for independence (many died) and won.
- The new technology which brought the information revolution, letting people no matter how far apart reach each other by the computer/internet.
- 911 saw America attacked and left shocked. They refuse to accept being infiltrated at home and still fight to regain respect in the changing world.
- The building of the Suez Canal that opened in 1869 after 10 years (that claimed lives of Caribbean workers) not for the further development of countries in the area but for strategy use by out-side forces (today there is talk about further development of the canal — extending it further).
- MANDELA (b-1918 and d-2013)

Freedom fighter ended in him being arrested in 1964.
Jailed and spent 27 years (released in 1990).
He went through the racist court system of apartheid.
Found guilty and spent confinement in prison.
(During the years most youths were developing into adults.)

His fight for the right to freedom continued
Creating the condition for others to enjoy some power, liberty and education.
But economical slavery remained in all non-white systems.

He also represented the struggle that African people endured around the world.
The system that was designed to keep non-white people in control
Telling us what to do and when it should be done (it was never suspended).

Nevertheless, continued by creating and developing new, sophisticated systems.
Systems of mental and economical slavery, preventing total freedom.
Note: Mandela, like all human rights leaders, was considered dangerous.

Most died at the hands of those who control our lives fighting for freedom. Like:
- Marie-Joseph Angelique, who was set on fire (1734 Montreal, Canada) for an incident (burning a town to the ground) she didn't commit (burning a town to the ground);
- Cuffy/ Kofi (led a slave rebellion) d. 1763 (Guyana);
- Sojourner Truth 1797-1833;
- Bussa (led the Bussa rebellion)-d. 1816 (Barbados);
- Paul Bogle 1820-1865 (Jamaica) hung because he wrote a letter to the Queen asking that she free the slaves;
- Harriet Tubman 1822-1913;
- Madam C J Walker 1867-1919;

- Daisy Bates 1914-1999;
- Gwendolyn Brooks 1917-2000;
- Rosa Parks 1913-2005;
- Ida B Wells 1862-1931;
- Toussaint L'Ouverture 1791-1804-killed (Haiti, the first African country to fight for independence from their British rulers);
- Nathaniel Turner 1800-1831;
- Patrice Lumumba 1925-1961 (Congolese Independence leader);
- Malcolm X 1925-1965;
- Fred Hampton 1948-1969;
- Soledad Brothers (Jonathan P Jackson 1953-1970/ George L Jackson 1941-1971);
- Steve Biko 1946-1977 (South Africa);
- Indira Gandhi (b-1917 d-1984) assassinated in India;
- Tubal Uriah Butler 1897-1977 (Grenada/Trinidad);
- Shirley Chisholm 1924-2005 (Barbados/USA).

READ/Listen to the lyrics of a song sung by
Billie HOLIDAY, "STRANGE FRUIT"
Which describes how life was in the South on Verve 1945-1959.

2014 HAVE FAITH

Have faith in daily undertaking in life.
Be it work, play, love, driving or walking.
We must keep faith alive.

2014 GOD

God is the same in any religion.
Called by different names.
All religion ends at the same road.
The belief is a heavenly creator who made us.
It is up to you to believe.

2014 PARENTS TEACHINGS RETURN

Thoughts
Advice that were told to us as youth
Returns to the present from the inner mind

Didn't make sense when first heard.
It was meaningless to us then.
Today they present themselves in the mind

Understood even if our elders have passed on.

2014 ABOUT A FRIEND

U just sitting there
Sorry for yourself
U don't know what U want.

Always listening to other people.
U have not made up your mind.
Come and see for yourself

What life is about in foreign countries?
Your problem is dealing with change.
It is tearing your mind apart.

U do not want to access changes
Don't want to leave the comfort
Of your place of bad memories.

2014 REMEMBER

U doing the same thing
Over and over
U get the same results.

U got visits
Trying to please U
U have no intention to leave

U are the first woman
Who is not ready.
To see where her family lives

U wait for some new problem
U drop the idea of coming
U have a new problem

U remain
It is getting worst for U
U are not yourself

U have not changed
U will be mad
U might never change

U will swear out loud
U have to be told
U have the truth.

2015 OLD AGE

Today I saw an old man being assisted.
A young female helped him off the subway
Guided by a helping hand to the platform
As a mother does with her small child.

Live really revolves in a circle.
We are born and as a child
Have to be guided by older adults.
We are later left on our own.

Adults see we are capable on our own
To endure life's daily ventures by ourselves.
Then we move through the three stages of life.
Child age, middle age and lastly old age.

As this stage we again become a child.
Being moved to live in a group home by family
Becoming dependent on loving humans for help
Waiting on time unlike the time of our birth.

Looking forward to growing into an adult
Waiting on the final stage in life
A stage we all have to take
Final, transition to the unknown, Death.

2015 LIVING WITH GHOSTS

We live with ghosts in the spiritual realm.
Although we don't always see or hear them.
Ghosts live in our minds from our past
Either from what was done
Or what others did to us in the past.

Ghosts memories live in most cultures.
Lingering ghosts of the enslaved captured.
African murdered and dehumanized.
Souls that are not at rest.
Leaving a terrible reminder of slavery

Which is still around in different clothing.
Some of the ghostly deeds have entered hearts.
Hearts leaving humans surrounded.
Surrounded in thoughts of darkness.
Built in many non-white cultures.

These souls like the dead souls.
Are left wondering. Why?

Left dragging sorrow like a heavy box.
Project on their faces.
And are told in stories or folk tales.

Ghosts in the Aboriginal culture are important
To the advancement of their future.
Stories dealing with survival in rugged terrain.
That is reference for their daily lives.
Or the evil strangers who entered their path.

Wicked colonial times lingering in the minds.
Enslaved people suppressed and controlled.
Lingering ghosts of the enslaved captures, murders.
And dehumanized souls killed and not at rest.
Leaving a terrible taste in the mouth of many.

Haunting those living and enslaved.
Ghosts also show up in marriages.
Two humans united by man and God.
Giving rise to two people united.
Living together with compounded stories.

Compounded hidden stories of differences.
Different ghost stories from their past.

2015 DREAM IN TRINIDAD

My friend had a lime.
All foreign friends attended.
Just before it started

A live wire fell in front of the house.
His father passed the wire in the trench.
O what a display we had.

Fire, steam, smoke and musical sounds.
An arrear of loud sounds bellowed
Coming from the wire and water.

After the display of hot wire in water
The lime continued with real music.
Trini sounds playing and filled the place.

The police showed up late to check
To make sure it was not the home.
A dream. Don't know why.

2015 MOTHER OR WIFE

Great Mothers
The head of loving families.
Display love and unity within their family.
Strive for total oneness in the family.

An important part of any family that is together
Know each in her family and teach and protect them.
Teach the older with good advice and the younger follow.
Understand her role and know about caring and loving.

MOTHERS WORRY
- WHEN THEY DON'T KNOW WHAT THEIR CHILDREN ARE DOING.
- WHEN THEIR CHILDREN DON'T TALK TO THEM AS THEY GET OLDER.

- About the relationship between a son and daughter.

- When they're grown-ups, a mother can only give advice.

2015 IMMIGRANT LIFE

This is the way it is.
Accepting foreign ID better
Saving money for trip.
Standing in line for passport
Getting it after fighting for a month

Dealing with red tape
In foreign office for visa
This is the way it is.
Accept foreign life
Sold by media and friends.

Buying needed stuff
For the first foreign trip
Ticket bought for trip
After setting date to leave
Time comes to leave

Feeling sad and unsure
Leaving your birthplace
Behind in the sun
Line-up starts in airport
Checking in, luggage, confused

New controlled system in play
Paying money and
Screening start
Before you leave the scene
Your heart beating fast

Being moved along
Then you sit and wait
To enter the plane
Leaving on Caribbean Jet
Leaving country of birth

Thinking all the time
Will they accept me?
Am I going to be returned?
Entering an unknown place
What would it be liked?

Can I adjust to the changes?
Plane landing
Confused
Long lines
Questions from officers

Feel like an outsider
Given a conditional chance to enter
Going through culture shock
Trying to adjust to changes
Applying for and getting plenty of cards

Government identity cards
Trying to accept different foods
Might die from hunger if I don't eat
No family to welcome me
Can't stay at friends anymore

Looking for an apartment to rent
Lord, it is expensive and not easy to find
Made plenty of moves in one month
With my grip and bag of food
Money running out, must find a job

To pay rent or I freeze to death
Winter coming and it's getting cold
Plenty of rules and requirements
To be employed in a foreign place
Meeting plenty of roadblocks

With the sudden changes to fit in
Suddenly starting to realize
Was told a lie about foreign life
Employment is a must
No employment lasts forever

Must pay rent that rises or evicted
Rising food prices and cost of living
Wages remain the same, no increase
Bills must be paid first
Before buying food to eat

Finding a true friend is hard
Another surprise arises
Being rejected and suppressed
Disliked and feared due to differences
- Language
- Culture
- Skin color

Can't handle it no more
No corporation from humans
People selfish
Can't deal with carding
Fear of walking on the road
Going back home to my Caribbean Country.

2015 SUMMER

Refugees and not BOAT PEOPLE.
The world stops sleeping.
Stop sleeping and looking.
Looking at what was ignored.
Ignored till a white child was found.
Lying on a beach, drowned.

Ignored before Obama took power.
African people had been seen fleeing.
Fleeing their political corrupted countries.
Fleeing in boats from war-ridden places.
In boats overfilled and drowning.

Drowning at sea in large numbers.
Drowning and the world didn't care.
Fleeing in search of a better life.
Better life from war and poverty.
They escaped but died at sea.

Died like the slaves during the slave trade.
They came from:
- African Continent
- Haiti
- Ethiopia
- Cuba
- Mexicans crossing into USA

They were called
- Boat people
- Sick and poor people
- People bringing diseases
- People that will take away jobs
- Not humans

- Murders
- Terrorists

No one cared about non-white people
Fleeing murder and violence.
No country wanted them
If they made to land were arrested.
Imprisoned and returned to their country.

Although
If one touched the land it was okay.
Wake up from your sleep
An alarm posted on television
A picture of a white child
Drowned and washed ashore
Picked up and held by a man

A white man holding the dead child
Wakes up the white world.
Started to help the refugees
Because of the white child image

White people changed their views
They became bewildered
No more THEM and US
But US and not THEM
They became humane

Today these new boat people
Are called
- Asylum Seekers
- Political Refugees
- Migrants

According to the Inter Press Services (2015-12-05)
Ethiopia has the biggest African refugee camps
Nobody is talking about it
There are 680,000 Africans in three camps

A microcosm of different people
From different part of Africa
- Yemen
- Guinea
- South Sudan
- Congo
- Uganda
- Somalia
- Eritrea
- Burundi and many more

How can humans be so unjust.

2016 CHANGING CUSTOMS

Umbilical cord
My father was like his father
When it comes to African customs
He buried my umbilical cord
In the yard where I was born

I was born at home
With the help of a midwife
I was a new link, new life
In the building of the next generation

My dear mother and father were full of joy
When I entered the world

My twin sisters had died, premature
Medical science wasn't equipped to keep them alive
I saw the hair and cord of my twin sisters
My father kept them in his drawer
He was in touch with the living dead

According to an African thought system
But did my father continue the custom
Like his father did?
Did my father bury the umbilical cord?
Of my sister and brothers who followed?

I don't know
And cannot get an answer
He and my dear mother
Died at an early age

To quote James Brown
I am African.
What African custom do I have?

My son was born
But I never saw his umbilical cord
Why did I not follow the African custom?
The system has changed us
It is now out of our hands
Modern technology has taken over.

2016 6:30 pm FRIDAY AFTERNOON

Sitting at the window

Taking it easy for once

The work week ended

Looking for a change

A different perspective

No controlled T V views

Looking at pedestrians

Passing on the sidewalk

A views less controlled

With some freedom

Humans can enjoy

A relaxing experience

My thoughts were interrupted

By a screeching sound heard

Penetrating my ear and mind

Stopping my moment of freedom

Making me wanting to know

What or where the sound came from

Looking and following the noise

It suddenly became apparent

A woman walking with bags

Created the repeated sound of rhythm

Returning home after buying food

Heavy shopping bags held in hands

Extending downwards to the ground

Heavy hanging bags below her waste

Hanging from short hands to the earth

Making screeching sound as she moves

Dragging along on the concrete pave

Creating musical sounds as she walks

Very short in statute near the ground

Shorter than me at 5ft 9ins in the air

Short and under four feet in height

Holding heavy bags in both hands

Longer from her folded fists downwards

Expanded with food stuff for daily meals

Never thought a woman of such statute

Could carry such a heavy heavy load

Guess if you have to do it you will

Carrying bags of heavy foods home

To cook and eat for a next week

Week of continual work one must endure.

July 4-2016 INSECURE MAN ON THE SUBWAY

Left night work
On the subway
Going home

Tired from work
9:30 am in de morning
Minding me business

The subway full with people
Some going to work
Some going home

Train stops
Man enters with a stroller
A young girl in it

Sitting like a queen
Innocent on her face
She makes eye contact

With a passenger
Her face lights-up
Smiling with the passenger

The man wants to know
Who the child is smiling with
Looks from the child to the person

Looking cross-eye and mad
There is bad intention on his face
He is full of anger

He moves the direction of the stroller
From facing the passenger to him
Cutting off the child eye contact

Between the child and passenger
Still mad and eying the passenger
With hard looks every minute
Fighting hard to interact
With the child in the stroller
Can't believe what I am seeing

Want to look at the passenger
But afraid of the angry man
He might turn on me

The train stops again
So I took a quick look
I got a big surprise

Seeing the passenger
It was a young white woman
The child was interacting with

The mother instinct in women
Always interact with children
People in the world really strange

Can't understand
Why the man was so up-set
About the interaction
Between woman and child.

ALSO BY Leyton Franklin

CARIBBEAN STORY SWEET, SWEET, SWEET

Caribbean Story Sweet, Sweet, Sweet is based on a 'middle-class' little boyin a 'big-house' which has another house on the parcel of land. The lower sections of the houses were rented creating a 'big-yard' with tenants living in limited space. Looking down from the window to the street, he was exposed to a collection of images and verbal expressions displayed by various characters of different ethnic and social backgrounds. His country people were referred to as low life, poor and bad elements for the ruling class. They were the working classes whose deplorable conduct his grandmother never wanted him to witness but he did. According to her the foul language and physical abuse of the lower class was derogatory and not conducive to her upper class society. She was also the owner and landlord of the houses situated at a busy intersection in the city. Explosions occurred also in the 'big-yard; daily mostly at the 'water-pipe' in the yard. Some of the tenants that he describes are:

- Mr. Roberson operated a cake-shop, a woman miser and wife abuser.
- Mr. Smith who lived with Miss. Marie that controlled him.
- The tailors who were involved in relationships with different women.
- Mrs. Samuels who had six children, living in a one-bedroom room.
- Doggy the boxer who was feared by men in the street and a con artist.
- Mohammed, East Indian Muslin married to a Portuguese woman and was always cussing.
- The goldsmith whose sons choke and robbed people.
- The man who thought no woman could catch him.
- The woman who was abused by her man.

Learn more at:
www.outskirtspress.com/
CARIBBEANSTORYSWEETSWEETSWEET

CPSIA information can be obtained
at www.ICGtesting.com
Printed in the USA
LVOW04s1043011116
511084LV00011B/63/P